The Lost Wallet

Written by
Rob Waring and **Maurice Jamall**

(with contributions by **Julian Thomlinson**)

Before You Read

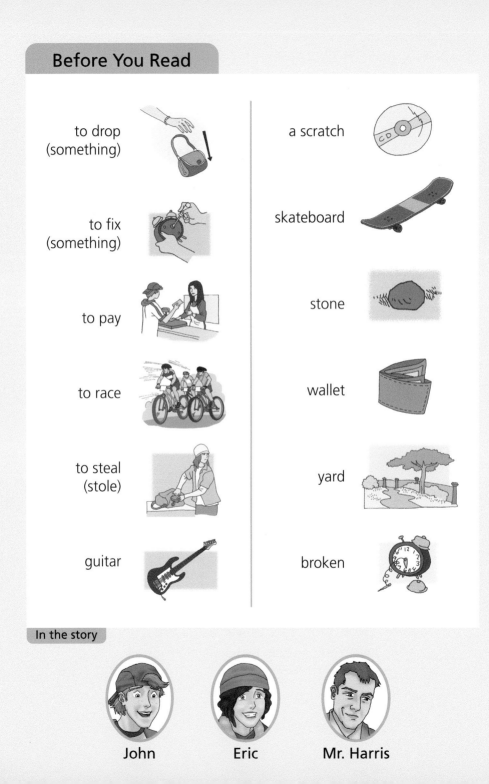

to drop (something)

a scratch

to fix (something)

skateboard

to pay

stone

to race

wallet

to steal (stole)

yard

guitar

broken

In the story

John

Eric

Mr. Harris

"Oh no!" said Eric. "Another test!" Eric and his best friend, John, were in Mr. Harris's class.

Mr. Harris spoke. "Yes, Eric. There's another important test tomorrow."

"But, Mr. Harris . . . ," said Eric. "We just had a test."

"Yes, I know. And your test was the worst in the class."

"But I don't have time to study. Can we have the test next week?" asked Eric.

Mr. Harris said strongly, "No, Eric."

"But . . ." said Eric.

"No way, Eric," said Mr. Harris. "Test! Tomorrow!"

After school, Eric and John were talking. "I hate Mr. Harris," said Eric. "Why does he give so many tests?"

John replied, "Yeah, I know. I hate tests, too. I don't like him either."

"Come on, John," said Eric. "Let's have some fun. I'll race you to the skate park." They often raced there.

"Sure," said John. "The slower one has to buy a drink."

"Okay, but I'll win. You can't win on that old skateboard of yours," said Eric. "Are you ready? Go!"

Eric and John raced to the park together on their skateboards.
Eric was faster than John. Eric saw a stone on the ground.
"John, look out!" said Eric. "There's a stone." John tried to
jump over the stone, but his skateboard hit it.
"Arghh . . . !" he said. John fell off his skateboard. He hit the
ground hard.
"Are you hurt?" asked Eric.

"No. I'm okay, thanks," John answered. Then he looked at his skateboard. It was broken.

"Look at my skateboard," said John. "It's broken!"

"Oh, no!" said Eric. "Now, you'll have to buy a new one."

John replied sadly, "I can't. I don't have any money."

"Well, let's go to the store. Maybe they can fix it," said Eric.

"Okay, let's go," said John. "But first, I have to buy you that drink."

Later, John and Eric went to the skateboard store. John asked the man, "Can you fix this?"

The man looked at the skateboard. "I'm sorry," he said. "I can't. Forget about this skateboard. You need a new one."

"Oh, I see," said John sadly.

Eric was looking in the music store window. He said, "Wow, John! Look at this guitar. I love it. But I don't have any money!"

John replied, "I know how you feel."

John and Eric walked to the bus stop. They were waiting for a bus. They saw a man. He was running for the bus.

"Is that Mr. Harris?" asked John.

"Yeah, but I don't care. I hate him," said Eric.

Mr. Harris had many things. When he was running for the bus, something fell onto the ground.

Eric and John saw it. Mr. Harris did not see it fall. He got on the bus and the bus left.

Eric and John went to look at it. "What is it?" asked John. "It's Mr. Harris's bag," replied Eric. He picked it up. "Let's look inside it."

"No," said John. "We shouldn't."

Eric did not listen to his friend. He opened the bag and looked inside. "Hey, there's a wallet. Maybe there's some money in it," he said.

"No," said John again. "Don't open it. It's not ours." But Eric opened the wallet.

They found a lot of money in the wallet!

"Wow!" thought Eric. He was very excited. "Look at all this money!" he said. "Teachers have a lot of money! I'm lucky! I can buy that guitar with this money!"

"What!!?" said John. "You want to buy the guitar? With Mr. Harris's money? But it's not yours!"

"Okay, okay," said Eric. "I know it's Mr. Harris's money. But nobody knows we have it. And we hate him, right? Nobody saw us, so we can keep it. It's ours now."

John just looked at his friend. He could not believe Eric. He said nothing.

Then Eric said quickly, "You can use the money to buy that new skateboard, too."

"I don't want to buy the skateboard with Mr. Harris's money," shouted John.

Eric replied, "Be quiet, people will hear you." He continued, "John, you hate him, too. He always gives us tests and too much homework."

"Eric!" replied John. "I know he gives us lots of tests. And I know he's not a nice man, but we shouldn't take his money!"

"But . . ." said Eric. "Look at all this money. He doesn't need it." Eric showed John the money.

John said, "Look, Eric. We should give his money back to him." He looked at Eric and said coldly, "I don't want to steal from anybody. It's not fair. Eric, I'm worried about you."

"Okay," said Eric. "I was only joking." John looked at Eric. He did not think Eric was joking.

Eric said, "Okay. So when do we give it back to him?"

"At school tomorrow," John said. "He's our teacher for the first class. Let's give it to him then."

Eric said, "Yeah. Great idea. Then maybe he won't give us the test!"

"Eric!" said John.

"Okay," said John. "I'll give the wallet to him tomorrow before class."

"Umm . . . No. I'll give it to him," said Eric. "I'll bring the wallet tomorrow. See you." He put the wallet in his bag. "I must be going now. I have to study for the test."

"Oh," said John. "Aren't you going to catch the bus?"

"Umm . . . No. I have to do some things in town," said Eric, smiling. "Bye."

"Oh, okay. See you tomorrow," said John. Eric walked away.

John was happy about Eric now. John thought, "I'm happy we're doing the right thing. We should give the wallet back. It's the right thing to do."

John got on the bus and watched Eric from the bus. Then he thought about Eric. "Eric said he had to study for the test. But that's very strange because Eric never studies for tests." John sat on the bus, thinking about Eric more and more.

On the bus, John started to worry about Eric. He thought, "What's Eric doing? Why was he smiling? What did he have to do in town? Something's wrong. He isn't usually this strange."

John remembered, "And he didn't want me to keep the wallet."

John thought for a long time about Eric. He was very worried.

Then he thought, "I'll call him. No, I'll go and see him later."

Later, John went to Eric's house. "I want to see if everything's okay with the wallet. I'm worried about Eric," John thought. "I hope he doesn't do anything wrong." John spoke to Eric's mother. "Umm . . . Hello, Mrs. Wilson. Is Eric in?"

"Oh hi, John. It's nice to see you. Are you here to play music with Eric?" she asked.

"Umm . . . music?" said John. "Umm . . . no."

"I see. Well, you can go up to his room," said Mrs. Wilson.

"Why did she ask me about music?" he thought.

Mrs. Wilson showed John to Eric's room. At Eric's door, John stopped. He could hear music coming from Eric's room. "That's strange. Eric's playing a guitar. But he doesn't have a guitar. What's going on?" John was very worried. Then he had a terrible thought. "Oh no. I hope he didn't . . ." He walked into Eric's room.

John was shocked. Eric had a new guitar. It was the guitar from the store!

"Eric!" John said.

Eric turned round and saw John. Eric was very surprised.

"What are you doing with that guitar?" asked John.

Eric's face went red. "Umm . . . Well, I bought it."

"You didn't buy it with Mr. Harris's money, did you?" asked John.

"Well . . ." said Eric.

Then Eric gave John a new skateboard. "What? You bought this for me?" asked John. "You used Mr. Harris's money for this, too, didn't you?"

"Well, yes. I did," said Eric, trying to smile. "You didn't have the money and you needed a skateboard, so I bought it for you."

"But it wasn't your money! I don't want it. Take them back to the store and get the money back," shouted John. He threw the skateboard onto the bed. The skateboard hit the guitar.

They looked at the skateboard and the guitar. They both had small scratches. Eric showed John the scratches. "Oh, no. Look at the scratches," said Eric. "I can't take them back to the store now."

Eric continued, "Look, John. Let's forget about this. Let's just keep the wallet. Then there won't be any trouble."

John saw the wallet on Eric's table. He picked it up.

"No, it's not our money!" said John angrily. "I'm going to give the wallet back to him tomorrow at school. I'm going home! Goodbye." John walked away.

The next day at school, John saw Eric. Eric spoke first.

"John," Eric said. "You're right, we should give it back. I was wrong to buy the guitar and the skateboard."

"Yes, I know!" said John. "You should take the guitar and the skateboard back to the store."

"Well . . ." said Eric. "I can't. The guitar and skateboard are scratched. They won't give me the money back."

Eric continued, "Look, John. Nobody knows we have the wallet. I know it was wrong. But we can't give back half the money. I think we should say nothing. It's easier than giving back half the money."

"No, Eric," said John. "We have to pay it back. It's not ours."
"But if we give it back, we'll be in big trouble. Do you understand?" said Eric.
John replied, "Yes, I know. It was wrong to do that, but it's wrong to keep it, too. I'm going to give it back."
Eric said, "But John, we may be in really big trouble. We can't give it back now. I'll work to pay Mr. Harris. Let's keep it a secret."
"No, that's too late," said John. "I'm going to give it back now." He walked out of the room.

John was very angry with his friend. "Why can't Eric understand?" he thought.

He walked to Mr. Harris's room, and then he stopped. He thought, "Eric is right. If I give it back to Mr. Harris, he will ask many questions. Then, I'll be in trouble. Eric will be in trouble. What can I do?"

Then he had an idea. "I know! I know what I can do," he thought. John smiled when he saw Mr. Harris's bag. He looked around. Nobody was there. He put the wallet back in Mr. Harris's bag.

Suddenly, there was a noise behind him. Mr. Harris saw John holding the wallet.

"What are you doing with my bag?" shouted Mr. Harris. John turned around and looked at Mr. Harris.

"Nothing!" said John. He was scared.

"What's that in your hand?" asked Mr. Harris. Then he saw the wallet in John's hand.

"That's my wallet. You stole it!" he shouted.

"No, I didn't," said John. "No, I was putting it back."

"Putting it back? I don't believe you," said Mr. Harris. "Come with me."

Mr. Harris took John to his room. He walked with John through the school. Everybody looked at him. They knew he was in trouble. Eric was shocked. He knew John was in big trouble, too. He knew why.

"Oh no. Mr. Harris caught John because of me," he thought. "Now he's in big trouble. What am I going to do? If I tell Mr. Harris, I'll be in trouble, too."

Eric watched him go into Mr. Harris's room.

"Sit down," said Mr. Harris. "I'm going to call your mother. She will take you home. Then I will call the police." John sat down and said nothing.

Mr. Harris called John's mother. "Hello, Mrs. Davies. This is Joe Harris from Bayview High School. Would you please come to school? I need to talk to you about John."

Then he called the police. He asked them to come to school.

Mrs. Davies came to Mr. Harris's room. Eric listened to Mr. Harris and Mrs. Davies.

Mr. Harris said to her, "I'm sorry to say this, but I caught John stealing my wallet."

"What? John? Stealing? I can't believe it!" she said. She looked at John. "Is this true, John?"

"No. I didn't steal the wallet," he said.

Eric felt very bad because John did not say Eric's name.

Mr. Harris said, "That's not true. You had my wallet in your hand. I'm sorry, but he must leave the school. We can't have boys like John at this school. The police are coming soon to take him away."

Mrs. Davies said, "I understand." She looked at John. She was very angry.

Just then, Eric came in the room. "Excuse me, Mr. Harris, I need to tell you something."

"Yes? What is it?" Mr. Harris asked.

"John and I saw you drop your wallet at the bus stop yesterday," he said. "John wanted to give the wallet back to you. But I didn't. I used your money and bought a guitar and a skateboard."

"What?" said Mr. Harris. "You used *my* money to buy a guitar and a skateboard?" He was really angry.

"Yes, I did. But John was very angry with me. He decided to give back the wallet. He didn't want to tell you because he would be in trouble. And there was only half the money. So he decided to put the wallet in your bag. But you caught him. I'm sorry, Mr. Harris. But I was the bad one. It wasn't John."

Eric turned to John. "I'm really sorry, John."

"Is this right, John?" asked Mr. Harris.
"Yes. Everything's true," said John. "I didn't tell you because I didn't want Eric to be in trouble."
"I see, well this is different," said Mr. Harris.
Eric said, "I'm sorry, Mr. Harris. I'll give the money back."
Mr. Harris replied, "Maybe. I must talk to the police first. We must decide what to do with you two boys. Go and sit over there."

The police came. "The police are here," John said to Eric. "Oh, no! Now we're really in trouble."

"We?" said Eric. "Not you, me! *I'm* in trouble. You did everything right. I got you into trouble."

"Yes, but . . . Well, thanks for telling Mr. Harris. You're a real friend, Eric," John replied.

Eric said, "That's okay. I was wrong to keep the wallet." He was very worried. "What's going to happen? Will we have to leave school?"

John replied, "I don't know. I really don't know." John was really worried, too.

The police officer and Mr. Harris came to John and Eric.
"We talked about the wallet and what you did," said the police
officer. "Mr. Harris decided you do not need to come with me.
He said he has another plan. I agree with it. You can go now."
"Thank you, Mr. Harris," said Eric. "I will *never* do that again.
I'm really sorry, Mr. Harris, Mrs. Davies, and John."
"That's okay," replied Mr. Harris.
John asked, "What's your plan, Mr. Harris?"

Eric and John were at Mr. Harris's home. They were working in his yard. They were working to pay the money back to Mr. Harris. Mr. Harris told Eric to work every weekend for 6 months to pay the money back.

John was helping Eric. "Do you need some help, Eric?" he asked. Eric replied to his friend, "Yeah, thanks buddy."